For Mark Rea, who listened to every draft, thank you.
—HD

For my family, who taught me to love being Japanese American.
—NG

RISING ABOVE

THE WATARU "WAT" MISAKA STORY

WRITTEN BY **HAYLEY DIEP**

ILLUSTRATED BY **NAOMI GIDDINGS**

No part of this publication may be reproduced, stored in a retrieval system, or transmitted in any form by any means, electronic, mechanical, photocopying, or otherwise, without the prior written permission of the publisher,

Triumph Books LLC, 814 North Franklin Street, Chicago, Illinois 60610.

Printed in China ISBN: 978-1-63727-477-4

62

years

ago.

That was the last time
Wataru "Wat" Misaka
stood in Madison Square Garden.

It never occurred to him then
that he had done
something historical.

Unknown.

The basketball soared through the sky—*swish!*

Wat Misaka, a young Japanese American born to immigrant parents, played basketball under the glow of stars and a small street lamp.

Unfair.

At fifteen, Wat became the man of his house.

Mom wanted to whisk him and his brothers back to her home in Hiroshima, Japan, but America was home to *Wat*. He said, "No, you can take my brothers and go, but I'm staying."

Mom chose to remain in their home in Ogden, Utah.

Unthinkable.

Thousands of miles away, Japanese airplanes struck Pearl Harbor with bombs and bullets.

Wat reeled in shock and confusion. *How could his parents' birth country attack his own like this?* he wondered.

People were angry.

Wat was sad.

America was at war.

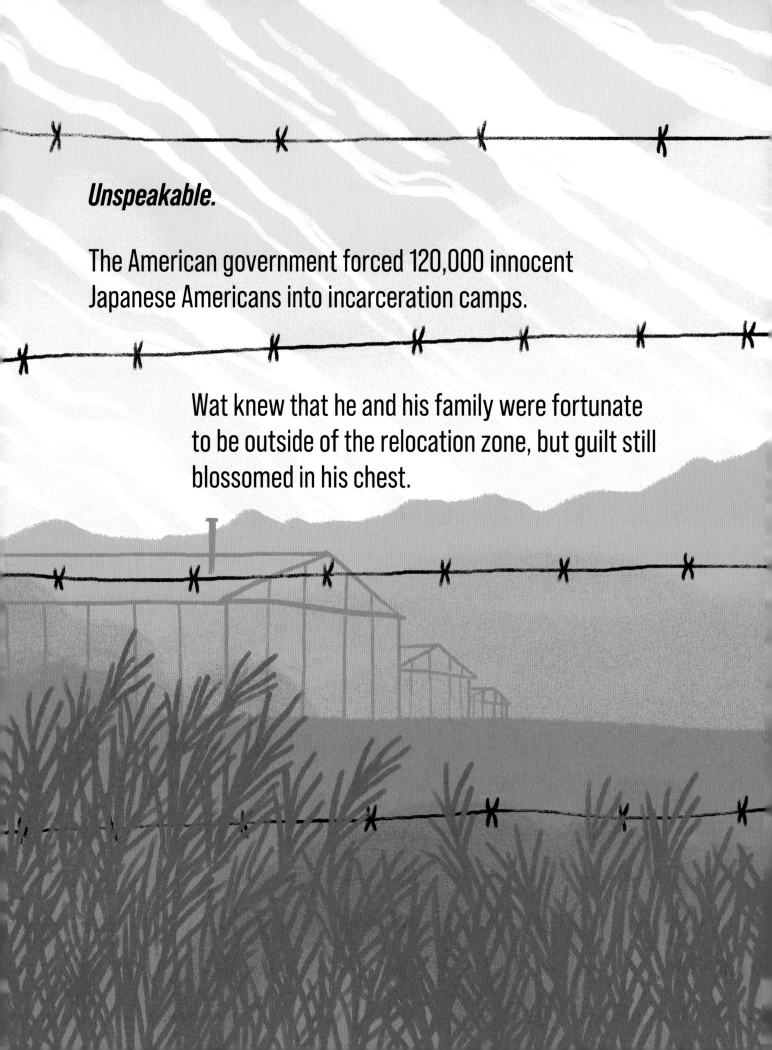

Unspeakable.

The American government forced 120,000 innocent Japanese Americans into incarceration camps.

Wat knew that he and his family were fortunate to be outside of the relocation zone, but guilt still blossomed in his chest.

He was free to study and play
basketball while his friends lived
and worked in camps.

Unjust.

Fans chanted, "go home" when Wat stepped onto the court.

This is my home, he thought.

Wat's teammates at the University of Utah viewed him as their equals. Teammates, like Dick Smuin and Arnie Ferrin, watched his back when they were on the road.

Together, they impressed crowds by playing fast paced basketball.

They were known
by many names: Cinderella Team,

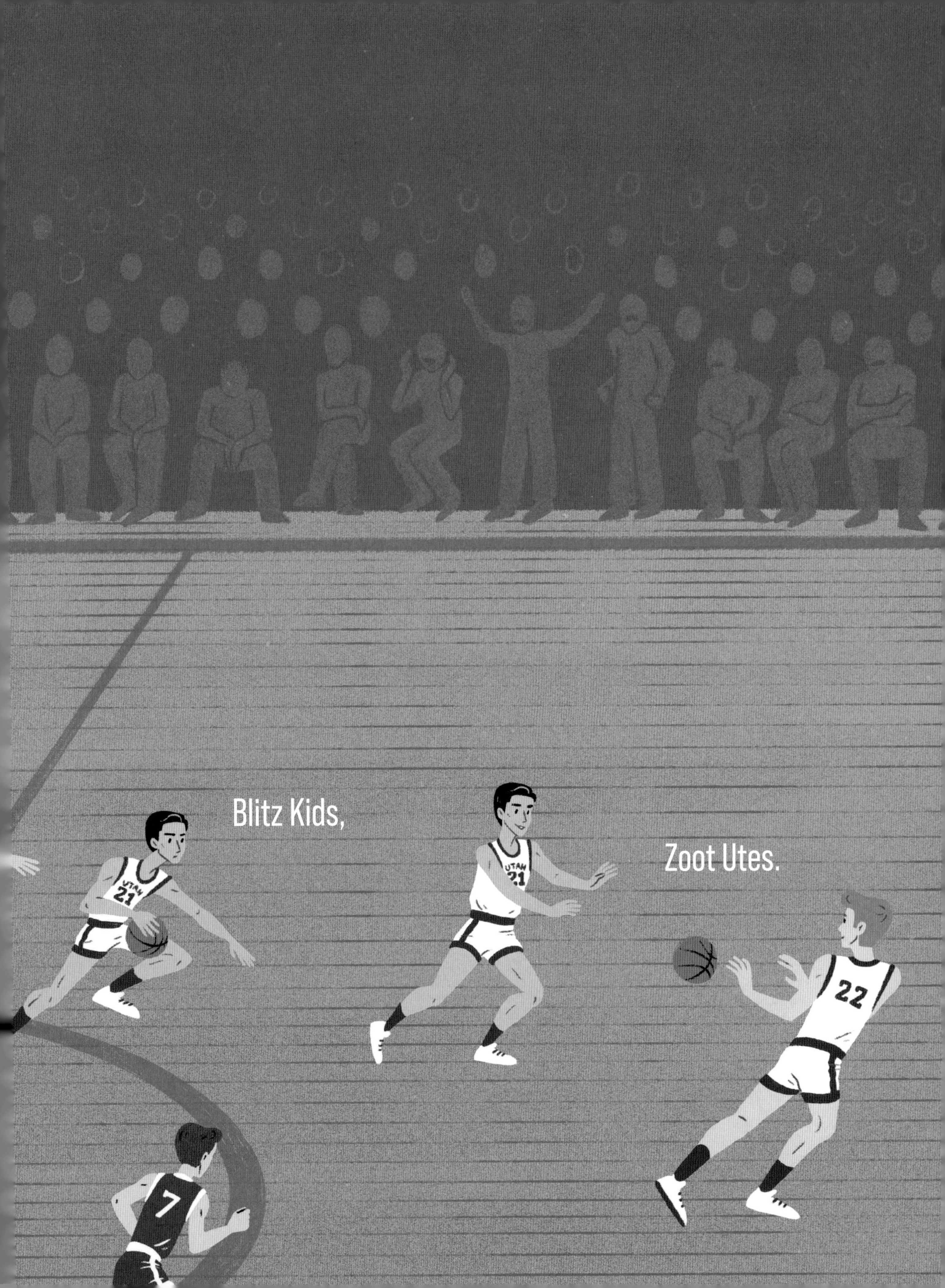

Blitz Kids,

Zoot Utes.

Underdogs.

Wat's basketball team won the 1944 NCAA championship. They traveled to Madison Square Garden and surprised everyone by defeating the NIT champions in a Red Cross charity event.

Fans cheered not only for Utah, but also for Wat's hustle and quick passes.

Wat could hardly believe his ears!

The Blitz Kids returned home to a parade of fans... and draft notices for World War II.

Unbelievable.

Atomic bombs dropped onto Hiroshima and Nagasaki, killing hundreds of thousands of Japanese people. Wat served in the U.S. Army and deployed to Hiroshima, Japan.

There, he felt unmoored, like
a man without a country.

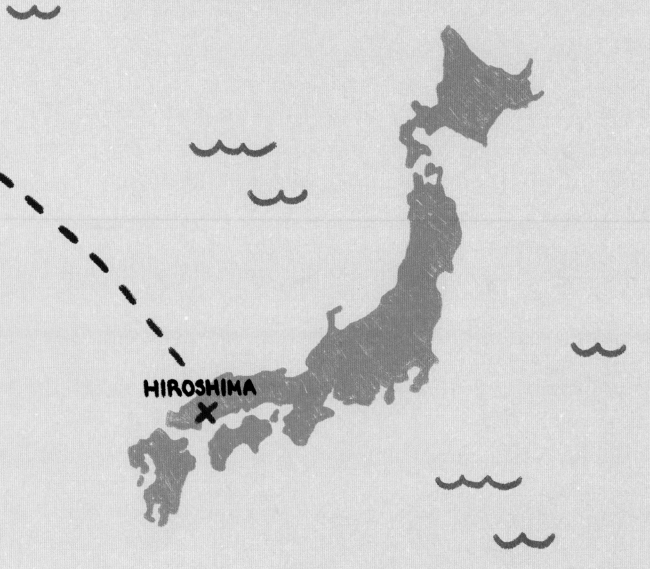

HIROSHIMA
X

In his uniform, he was hated by the Japanese.
Without his uniform, he was mistrusted by fellow
Americans. Wherever he turned, he was an enemy
in somebody's eyes.

Undeniable.

After two years of military service, Wat returned
to the University of Utah. His teammates were
automatically accepted back onto the starting team.
He was required to try out.

Wat charged up and down the court, reminding the coach of his skills and worth.

Unrelenting.

The Cinderella Team returned to Madison Square Garden to face the Kentucky Wildcats in the NIT 1947 championship game.

Wat's teammate, Arnie Ferrin, sank one-handed shots and underhand lay-ups.

Wat blocked shots and snatched up passes, limiting the player of the year to scoring only one point with his tight defense. Utah won the NIT championship.

"Go Wat!" fans chanted.

That night fans saw Wat for who he was: *a basketball player.*

Ned Irish, president of the New York Knicks, drafted Wat Misaka onto the Knicks.

Wat became the first person of color to play in the NBA. The Knicks hoped that Wat would bring cheering fans to their stands.

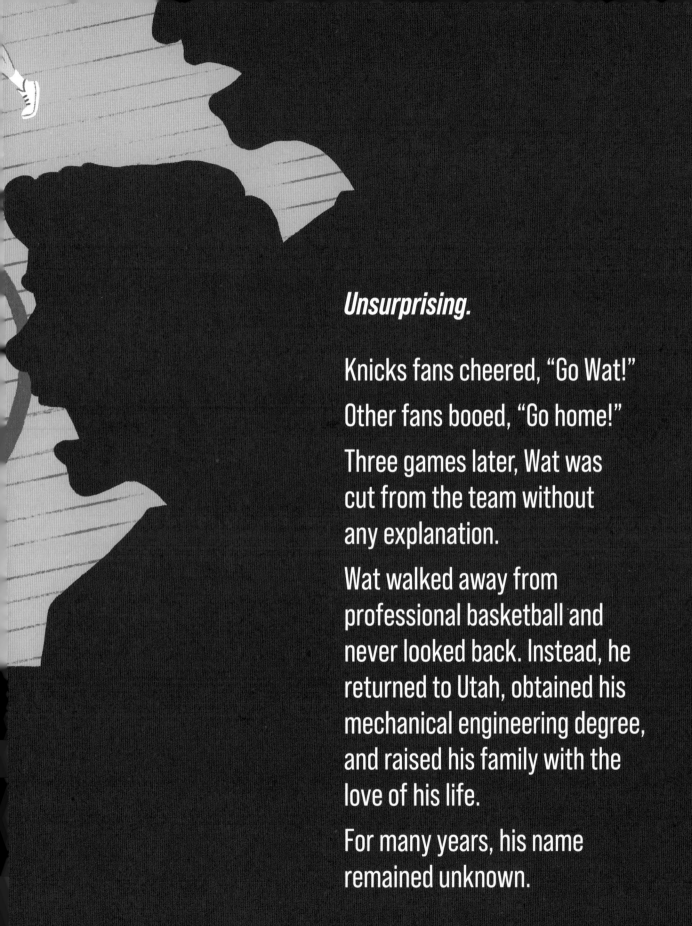

Unsurprising.

Knicks fans cheered, "Go Wat!"

Other fans booed, "Go home!"

Three games later, Wat was cut from the team without any explanation.

Wat walked away from professional basketball and never looked back. Instead, he returned to Utah, obtained his mechanical engineering degree, and raised his family with the love of his life.

For many years, his name remained unknown.

Unforgotten.

Here he stands, decades later, in Madison Square Garden.

The Knicks honor him with a Number 15 jersey—*his jersey*.

Wat's basketball career may have been short-lived, but he now understands its significance.

Wataru Misaka, a Japanese American born to immigrant parents, has shown the world that anything is possible.

Undefeated.

Author's Note

During a time when nearly all of America mistrusted and mistreated Japanese Americans, Wataru Misaka demonstrated courage and strength by stepping onto a basketball court and not allowing racism to discourage him from playing a sport he loved. Although he walked away from the sport when he was cut from the Knicks, his actions mirror an unfortunate reality for many marginalized people in America: sometimes it is okay to walk away and find a new path.

I hope that readers find Wat's story both interesting and inspiring. I know I did.

Wat's children, Nancy Umemura and Hank Misaka, shared that while Wat's basketball career with the NBA, then known as the BAA, was short-lived, Wat lived a long and fulfilling life. After the Knicks, Wat turned down the opportunity to play basketball with the Harlem Globetrotters, returned to Utah to marry his sweetheart, Katie, and finished his degree.

With his wife's support and love, Wat lived the life he'd always wanted. He remained good friends with his teammates from University of Utah, played golf, bowled, and went backpacking in his free time.

Thank you Callie, Ken, Sharon, Kim, and Sophie for all of your feedback and support. Thank you to the Misakas and Johnsons for your valuable insight. Thank you to my family and friends for your love and patience. Thank you to Naomi and the Triumph team for making this book possible. —HD

Thank you to the Misakas and Johnsons for their generosity, Britt Siess and Julia Kuo for their guidance, and Hayley and the Triumph team for their collaboration. Thank you to my family for their help with Nikkei history, Utah skylines, and more. And thank you to Nikolai, for everything else. —NG

Transcending: The Wat Misaka Story was a documentary created by Bruce and Christine Johnson. The majority of the information for this book was gathered from that documentary and from speaking with Bruce Johnson and Wat Misaka's children, Nancy Umemura and Hank Misaka.

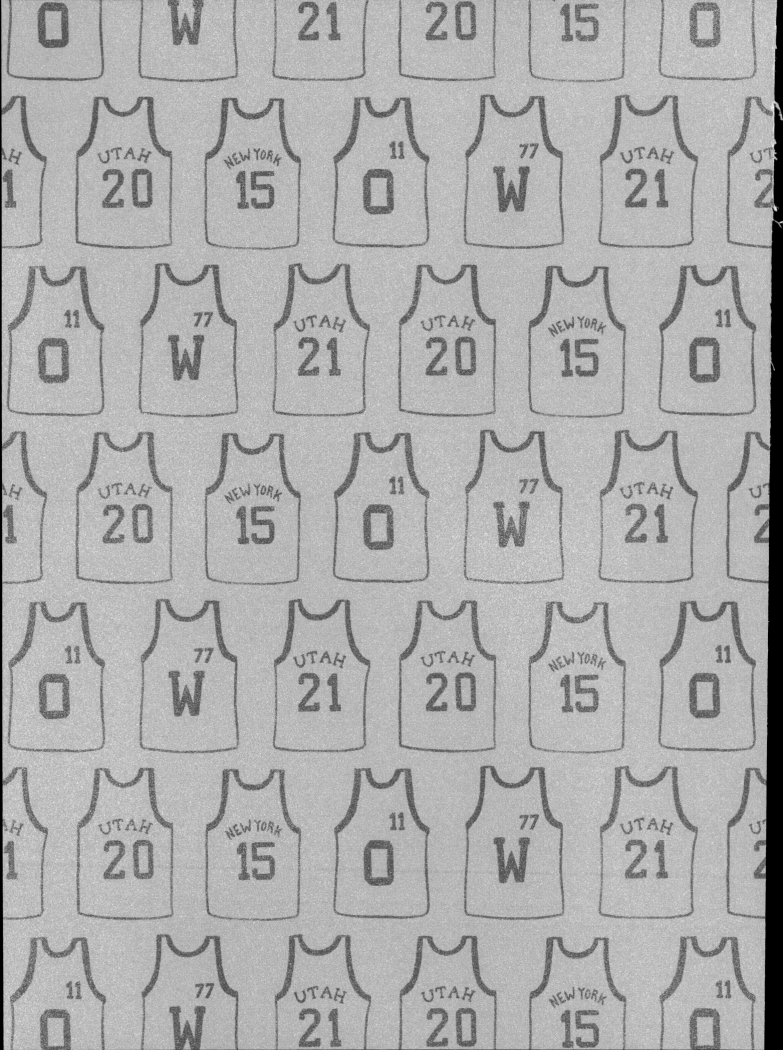